"I wish I had read "
– E. Lee Walker, F
Aι

FAST START to CAREER SUCCESS
Making the Most of Your First Job

An Executive's Advice
to His Children:
36 Tips You Did NOT
Learn in School

Ron Kurtz

outskirts
press

Dedication

To my incredible children, Carrie Kurtz Turner and Jason Kurtz, who have been highly successful in their personal and professional lives. To my wonderful wife Betty, who has been supportive despite the hardships and inconveniences she experienced because of my focus on work and career during our first 50 years of marriage. I love them all very much. I am proud of them.

Acknowledgements

This book would not have been written without the encouragement and help of both Carrie and Jason. I cannot thank them enough. They spent a lot of their valuable time helping me with this book. They are my pride and joy.

I want to acknowledge several executives who have been very important to my development and career. Among those who have passed away, (and the places where we were colleagues), I have great memories of Jean-Claude Potier (the French Line, Club Med, and Windstar Cruises), Marty Marshall (Harvard Business School professor), and Fred Mayer (Regent, Commodore, and Crown Cruise lines).

Others who taught me lessons described in this book include Tom Rader (three separate railroad vacation concepts), George Myers (various Caribbean projects), Dan Colussy (Northeast and Pan Am airlines), Helge Naarstad (Norwegian Cruise Lines, Sea Goddess Cruises, and World of ResidenSea), and Maurice Wiener (various real estate and entrepreneurial projects).

I owe a debt of gratitude to all of these executives.

Finally, I want to acknowledge Tucker Cox for his extensive help in drafting, editing, and organizing this book. He has a sharp eye for detail, a broad vocabulary, and impressive creativity.

Table of Contents

Introduction

I did not write this book for personal recognition or to praise my children. Carrie and Jason encouraged me to write this book. ***They believe the advice in it helped them in their first job and throughout their career and that it will help YOU too.***

For background, the **Appendix** presents a brief timeline of my education and career history as well as that of Carrie and Jason.

In *"**The Situation**"* section that appears after each tip, you will find examples of how Carrie and Jason applied my advice or later saw its relevance. They referred to this advice from time to time throughout their careers.

When Jason and Carrie graduated from college and accepted a job in the field where they wanted to build their career, I gave them these tips in the form of a simple, old-fashioned list. I wanted them to be successful and to benefit from what I learned during my life's work. Carrie and Jason's first real job began after college, but this advice applies to any career-oriented position you accept after finishing college or graduate school.

I wrote this book specifically for those beginning their first job to discuss typical concerns and anxieties and to correct myths about organizational life. The book provides insights that are not taught in school and that most parents rarely think to share from their own experience.

You will learn how to:

- make the most of your personal attributes

- work and interact effectively with other people within and outside of your organization

- be pro-active in taking advantage of challenges and opportunities that arise and

- keep your work and personal life in balance.

Your first job is a time to learn and to develop good habits and intuition for making the right decisions in the future. Presenting topics you did not learn in school, this book gives practical advice on using your first job to build a foundation for future career success. It reveals how to succeed throughout your career by working and interacting effectively with other people. It will help you advance faster.

The book discusses my personal experience, not the formal education and training I gained while earning my MBA degree at Harvard. These 36 tips represent simple common sense I learned and applied during my 20-year career as a corporate executive and 14 years as a management consultant.

Many of the tips relate in one way or another to making a good impression on your bosses and keeping them happy. Pleasing the boss had a big influence on my career path. Counting permanent positions and major consulting projects, I was hired three or more times by each of four different executives.

These four executives kept me busy for most of my career, which included the position of President of two cruise lines, one of which was a start-up, and Chief Marketing and Sales Officer of two other cruise lines, one of which was the industry's largest.

These four executives, together with two others who each hired me twice, represent most of my career and demonstrate the importance and rewards of keeping your boss happy.

While preparing examples for this book, my son and daughter said they had often implemented some of this advice instinctively. They felt like the tips were in the back of their mind (almost subconscious reminders) and had helped them form good instincts.

In other words, the book instills habits that are of immediate value to you in your first real job and throughout your career. The book is not limited to business people. It helps anyone who works in an organization. The advice applies to those in nonprofit, government, professional, and other environments. The advice is not just for college graduates. It helps anyone leaving school to take their first real job and start a career.

This book is not about how to find a job, how to prepare a resume, or how to act in an interview. It contains no theories of management, organizational concepts, work styles and habits, personality traits, or similar topics presented in many articles and books as "secrets of career success."

The book provides insight and practical advice that people often overlook or forget. It is a fast and easy read. It contains no heavy conceptual material that must be carefully analyzed and considered.

Make your first read a quick one. Do another read, this time slow and thorough, to reinforce your recall of the main ideas. Then, keep the book handy for reference when you face a challenge or when you want a reminder or need advice for an important situation on the job. Make this book one of your Go-To Manuals for managing your career. Allow the advice to become instinctive, as it did for Jason and Carrie.

Summing up, this book gives you advice and information you can use to do your job well: contribute to your team, listen and learn, support your boss, lead, take responsibility for your career advancement, participate in your industry, uphold good ethics and, all the while, be your authentic self.

Improving your competencies in these areas gives you job satisfaction and gratifying relationships with your peers, those you supervise, and your superiors. Gaining experience and skill in these activities qualifies you *to advance your career* to positions of more responsibility and compensation, either at your current employer or another company or organization. This book emphasizes that a fundamental part of career success is achieving a healthy, enjoyable work-life balance.

In a nutshell, this book is about doing your job well to be considered for promotion. Finally, as you accept that well-earned promotion or assume a new position in a different organization, review this book. With a new job, more responsibilities, and new challenges, the value of this book increases. Some of the tips are more useful for the road ahead than the one you left behind. Some Situations illustrate your current environment better than others. Make this book your career companion.

Chapter 1 ...
Be a Team Player

A successful organization is a team, with each team member having a role to play and contributing to the team's success. There will be times when you compete with a peer for recognition or your department has interests that conflict with another workgroup. It is best to have a friendly resolution of such differences. Avoid office politics and making enemies.

Keep the interests of your company as the top priority. View your personal interests and goals from the perspective of what is good for your organization.

These 6 tips for being a good team member helped me to keep my boss happy.

1. *Present ideas and proposals that are good for the team or the organization. Avoid offering ideas or taking actions that others*

see as self-serving; for example, recommending a sales incentive plan that may be particularly good for you but not in the company's best interests.

The Situation – soliciting input and listening pave the way to achieving company goals

Jason was asked to create a new sales team at one of his companies. The new team negatively impacted the existing sales team by taking away some of their key accounts, sales staff, and other functional departments in the company as well. To avoid the appearance of pursuing a self-serving reorganization, Jason spent time with sales and other leaders affected by a new sales team to discuss his vision and listen to their ideas and concerns. Though it might look like "good politics" to some, soliciting their input and listening to their concerns made the organization and new team's ultimate success much easier to achieve.

2. *Spend the company's money and use its resources as conservatively as if they were your own. Be as concerned about the company's profitability as if you owned it.*

The Situation – keeping a sharp eye on expenses increases profits

On Jason's first business trip, he noticed the airfare was much higher than he would typically expect. He discovered that the company booked flights close to departure day when fares are at their highest. He suggested to his supervisor that travel can often be anticipated and reserved well in advance when prices are much lower. His boss thanked him for his concern about company profitability but said having flexibility to choose the right person for the job at the right time had a higher priority than the incremental cost savings. Nevertheless, Jason's concern for company profitability made a good impression on his supervisor.

3. *Never justify a promotion or a raise based on your financial need or what other people earn. Justify a request for a raise by showing the contributions that you are making to the company. Promotions result from mastering your current job and demonstrating your ability to help the company even more by having more responsibility. You should already be performing at the next level before being promoted to it.*

The Situation – perform in your current job at the next higher level

Today information about a colleague's salary is more common because it is shared personally and occasionally published on websites. Most companies have processes that outline promotion and raise cycles.

Your manager might be put in a difficult situation if you make a request outside the established timing guidelines.

One option is to ask for your manager's feedback on another opportunity at higher compensation that has become available to you. This allows your supervisor to look at the context of the total package and to advocate on your behalf. Jason occasionally used this approach with success.

If you know a promotion cycle is approaching, make a case that you are performing work at a grade above your current position. My son earned an early promotion by using the metrics of a job at the next higher level to show what he did and how much extra revenue he produced from a consulting assignment.

After a year with his company, Jason knew a promotion cycle would occur soon. He was performing work as a team and client manager, which was at a level above his current position. He had sold additional work to the client, which was not a metric for his current role but rather for the next level up. Jason got his promotion after showing how much incremental revenue and profit he had produced.

Carrie emphasizes asking for a raise when you can show you have earned it. Do not base a raise request on a personal need, for example, an increase in your rent. During Carrie's new employee group orientation, the moderator noted, "you will know you are ready for promotion when you are already performing at the next level." At performance review time, Carrie knew if a promotion was coming if she had successfully performed responsibilities at a level beyond those of her peers.

4. *Avoid involvement in office politics. Avoid interdepartmental rivalries. You never know who your next boss will be. Seek to identify the winners and rising stars and work to develop a rapport with them. You can do this by offering to help them, particularly on tasks they may not want to do, and by seeking their advice. People always like to give their opinions.*

Connect with those who know more than you do and thus have much they can teach you. In your first job, you can learn from everyone, including what not to do. Throughout your career, there will be people who have knowledge and experience that can help you. Most people want to share their expertise. For example, if you are in product development you may ask a sales manager to assess a proposed product feature.

The Situation – understand how others feel about ideas, concepts, changes, and organizational performance

Watch for people who pursue a self-serving agenda in what they do and say. Chances are they are playing office politics. For instance, they may advocate new expense tracking software about which they know little, except that friends in the accounting department want to use that application.

As a rule, Jason believes doing what is best for the company will automatically avoid politics.

But do not confuse politics with understanding how others feel about ideas, concepts, changes, and organizational performance. Some may consider soliciting the opinions of others political. It is not. This knowledge helps you learn how to get things done in a company.

At the television network, Jason made an early effort to meet people in other departments of the company to learn what they did and how he interfaced with their role. In a meeting with someone in the sales department, he was fascinated to learn how their customers felt about his department's programming.

5. *Keep debates or disagreements focused on the business issue. Do not make it personal. Help the other person find a face-saving way out of their position so they can support you.*

The Situation – respect the point of view of others

In a meeting, Jason encountered considerable opposition to a proposal he advocated. Jason gave the opposition a face-saving way to change their position by suggesting he would agree with them if it were not for new data he had, and perhaps they might not have seen. The opportunity to consider new information led to support for Jason's recommendation.

6. *Show respect for and be friendly with Executive Assistants, Office Administrators, Analysts, and people at lower levels of the organization. Often, they are a source of helpful information about what is happening before it becomes common knowledge. Executives ask their Assistants their opinion of others, including you, making their Assistants influential in management's perception of your contribution to the organization. You would be surprised how frequently executives ask their Executive Assistants for their impressions and what they hear about people in the company.*

Though not as common as in the past and perhaps not called "executive assistants," where they do exist, people in this job and other administrative staff are important parts of the organization.

The Situation – build relationships at all levels in the organization

In his first job, Jason saw that Executive Assistants gave input on what roles new hires had in the company and participated in meetings where executives decided on new assignments.

Executives often ask their assistants what time staff arrive at the office in the morning and leave in the evening. My son's Executive Assistant interacts with every potential job candidate for scheduling, booking travel, and coordinating office interviews. Jason asks his assistant for feedback on the candidate. Is the candidate respectful? Friendly? Positive? Is the candidate a good cultural fit?

Having worked as a recruiter for a management consulting firm, Carrie participated in the administrative side of the organization. After interviewing the candidate, managers making a new hire decision always asked Carrie to assess the person and how the individual related to her. Decision makers had no interest in a candidate who did not respect people at every level of the organization.

Chapter 2....
Be a Listener
(and Learn)

Being a good listener is essential to identifying and correcting your areas needing improvement, understanding your colleagues' opinions, and gaining support or countering opposition to your ideas and proposals. Be prepared to acknowledge responsibility if you make a mistake, accept others' ideas, and learn new skills.

Listening is critical to learning, which you should never stop doing. Almost always, it is better to listen before you speak. The following 4 tips will help you keep your boss and colleagues happy.

7. *Accept criticism with grace and appreciation. Explain your position when appropriate, but don't risk appearing defensive. Accept feedback as a gift.*

The Situation – what can you do to improve?

"Thank you for your feedback" is one of Carrie's favorite lines. From that starting point, you have various options, such as asking what you can do to improve, requesting a model of a better approach, and soliciting help (which is always acceptable).

When your supervisor gives you a performance review, it is their job to provide feedback on what you do well and the skills and work habits you need to improve. Everyone can benefit from critical feedback, as no one is perfect. Don't make it difficult for your supervisor, who may be uncomfortable suggesting areas that need improvement.

In an early review in his first job, Jason's supervisor told him he was not as creative as other employees. Recognizing he lacked the experience to be one of the best, my son asked his supervisor the name of the person he thought was the most creative so that he could learn from him or her. Pleased the discussion was over and that Jason showed initiative to improve, the supervisor relaxed, grinned, and gave Jason a name.

8. *Remember, you are not the only one with good ideas. Create a nurturing environment that encourages people to make suggestions. Be open to the good*

> *proposals of other players. Even if their opinions are not up to par, give your teammates a fair chance to explain their position.*

Be tactful and informative when declining others' proposals. Always start with recognition of the good points of their suggestions. When possible, urge the person to refine their recommendation so that it can be used. Encourage him or her to make new proposals. Give people credit for their idea, even if you must substantially refine it to make it work. This advice gains more importance over time as you advance and have a team to supervise.

The Situation – be open to all (different) ideas

As they became team leaders, Carrie and Jason recognized it was not their responsibility to have the best ideas. They saw their role as facilitating the identification and development of solutions from members of the team, by creating an environment that encourages people to contribute thoughts, options, and innovations. At one level, all ideas are good ideas.

In a planning meeting with his team at an early stage in the Covid-19 pandemic, Jason's objective was to encourage thinking about their strategic direction for the next two or three years. At the start of the meeting, Jason reminded everyone that all ideas are good ideas and that the team should be creative and bold in their thinking about the future.

Several team members proposed excellent ideas that were quickly adopted. One proposal identified ways to collaborate and share information with team members while working remotely during the Covid-19 pandemic.

9. *Be careful about presenting your recommendations as surefire winners, particularly until you have gained some experience and maturity. Be enthusiastic, within limits, about your proposals. Present them for consideration and review by those with more experience and authority. Acknowledge weak points of your recommendation (hopefully with a way to offset them) as part of your presentation.*

You might test your ideas on peers or people in other departments before running them up the chain of command. Use this technique to identify the drawbacks of your proposal (and people will always find negative aspects) so that you can develop explanations to overcome likely objections. When you alert people to a potential problem or concern, be prepared to offer a possible solution. Avoid leaving others with a problem but no answers for corrective action.

The Situation – you do not own the best ideas

When Carrie has a candidate that she feels is a shoo-in for a position, she tempers her enthusiasm. She does not want the hiring manager to think she does not fully understand what they seek in a candidate. She balances being confident with being overconfident.

Jason believes the best solutions come from colleagues providing input from their different perspectives, making 1+1=3. He bounces his ideas off others and encourages others to bounce their ideas off him. In his first job at ESPN, he found himself stumped about how to proceed with a feature story with several possible angles. Discussing the program segment with a friend and colleague, Jason saw a way to present the information in a format that earned many compliments from senior management.

10. *Learn new skills that make you more productive. Attend training seminars and conferences in your company and industry when they offer the opportunity for more success in your current position or in the next job you've set your sights on. Watch for other venues for learning and self-improvement. These activities can make you more valuable to your boss and your company and are thus key to advancing your career. Take advantage*

of being new in a company (the honeymoon period) by asking questions to learn from everyone you meet.

Train to be an excellent communicator, both verbally and in writing, two skills essential to becoming a leader. Everyone has abilities, aptitudes and talents that can be improved, even the CEO. Self-awareness and objectivity about your strengths and weaknesses lead to understanding what needs improvement and planning to proactively strengthen your development.

Verbal skills are essential in many different settings, including presentations to large audiences. I was fired once in my career. The reason? My boss felt I did not make good presentations to big groups. After that experience, I encouraged my son and daughter to take the Dale Carnegie public speaking courses. They did so reluctantly but subsequently said they benefitted from this training by strengthening a skill vital to their performance and advancement.

The Situation – take advantage of your Honeymoon!

One of the best things about being new in a company is that you can ask any question, and everyone is generally happy to help. Take advantage of this "honeymoon period." Jason started his first job on a temporary six-month contract. During his honeymoon, he asked people for advice about what it took to be successful and hired permanently. Jason was amazed by others' willingness to help and share their experience, including an unexpected session of career advice with a network television program anchor who was putting on makeup in the men's restroom!

Chapter 3....
Be Your Boss's Star

You can do several things to keep your boss happy and be your boss's Most Valuable Player. Your boss should be confident that you will protect her from problems and do the good work that is expected of her team.

You need not resort to false flattery, endorsing all of the boss's ideas, or doing personal tasks such as collecting her dry cleaning. You do need to help the boss achieve her goals efficiently and effectively. She needs to trust that you will support and protect her interests.

Here are 4 tips you can follow to be an MVP.

    11. *No matter how menial the task assigned to you, accept it with a positive attitude and give it your best effort. You will get increasingly important and complex*

assignments as you demonstrate that you can do lesser ones on a quality basis.

The Situation – all work can be good work

Carrie's first job was in the trust operations department of a regional bank. This department was a training ground for recent college graduates hoping to use it as a stepping-stone to another role. Management selected Carrie to join a project team working on the merger of two regional banks.

The team consisted of vice presidents from both banks. Though Carrie had the title of Project Analyst, her role was primarily taking notes in leadership meetings. She took them with pride and care, in addition to her other responsibilities. After six months, Carrie had developed relationships with senior leaders of the organization, having shown her willingness to do the menial work, while also exhibiting her other skills. She earned a promotion to Project Manager.

12. *When you accept an assignment, make sure you understand what your boss wants you to do. Be willing to ask questions or to seek greater insight. It is best to admit you don't know or comprehend something instead of going in the wrong direction. However, be sensitive to the fact that people often give an assignment*

> *without knowing what they really ex-*
> *pect. Probe too much and you can put*
> *them in an embarrassing situation.*

When the desired end product is not clear, you have to take a chance: guess what the right thing is and then try to do it. Be prepared to have made the wrong assumption, to have your work changed or told that you need to do it differently. Do not take this personally or show a defensive attitude. Bosses often find that they can respond to a work product they are given better than they can initially provide clear direction.

The Situation –vague assignments can be opportunities

It is important to understand you might get an assignment that your boss has not fully defined. Do not let this situation or feedback that changes your initial direction frustrate you. Often it is easier for your supervisor to react to a semifinished product, as he or she may not know what the final deliverable looks like when initially asking you to do the job.

On Jason's first consulting project, the project team was redesigning the client's sales, marketing, and customer service departments. Jason, who was working on sales, was given few details about what was expected to be the final product. He took a first pass at the deliverable template and shared it with the project manager. In response, the manager expressed appreciation for the "trial" and suggested edits and tweaks that led to the document's final version. The result was shared with the other team members and became the basis of consistent, structured output for the client.

13. *Volunteer for additional work or do tasks others do not want. This (volunteering) is related to item #11 above. Take advantage of every opportunity to show your skills and a positive attitude.*

The Situation – rise up and volunteer!

There are always tasks to do outside of daily routine operations. Managers love volunteers who assume this work. However, keep in mind the importance of completing the undertaking properly.

In his first job, Jason volunteered to help a rising star put together a weekly Monday morning show that presented highlights from the weekend's football games. His task involved the tedious work of tracking down videos scattered around the office and researching certain facts. Jason's maintenance of a positive attitude and his offer to help were acknowledged and appreciated by both the rising star and the management team.

14. *Make a point of understanding your boss and what motivates her or him. Be supportive at all times and protect your boss from bad surprises or problems. Bypass or go above your supervisor's head to their boss as a last resort and in the most serious circumstances (something illegal, unethical, or immoral).*

The Situation – know what makes your supervisor tick

There may be occasions when you are doing work for different supervisors at the same time. There will always be instances when you start a new role with a new supervisor. Understanding your supervisors' motivations and priorities – and there are almost always differences – helps you perform better and meet their expectations.

In his first job, Jason worked on three projects for three different supervisors at the same time. One was a "gripper" who stressed out until he could see all the content come together for a show. Another focused on being as creative as possible. The third was a "perfectionist" who wanted no factual errors. Understanding the different agendas of each enabled Jason to tailor his work style to their requirements.

Chapter 4 ....
Be a Leader

You need not be a boss to be a leader. Leadership results from earning the trust and confidence of your colleagues. Set an example in attitude and actions that others will want to adopt or follow. Offer compliments and encouragement to others. Define a path forward when the direction is unclear.

Being a leader among your peers is a valuable contribution that will help keep your boss happy and get you a promotion. Here are 6 tips for earning a leadership role.

15. *Show self-confidence. Do not be arrogant or overbearing, which your peers will resent.*

The Situation – step up to the plate and take a swing, keeping your eye on the ball

In his first job, where it was perhaps best to be modest, Jason showed leadership by creating a plan to complete an assignment. Presenting such a plan to your supervisor inspires confidence that you know what you are doing and have things under control. Struggling to communicate how you are going to get the job done makes your supervisor nervous.

Jason developed and revised as necessary action steps for weekly assignments. The supervisor reviewed and tweaked the plan and received status reports every couple of days. The process instilled confidence in Jason's performance and competence, leading to more important assignments.

16. *A carrot motivates people better than a stick. No one is perfect and no one likes to be reminded of their imperfection. Use every opportunity to offer encouragement and to compliment and congratulate people on a job well done, even if they are your rivals or peers.*

The Situation – build relationships by complimenting others on their work

Some bosses lead by fear and intimidation (the stick). Others are more complimentary and encouraging (the carrot). You probably prefer to work for the latter and would be more loyal to them. It takes little effort to compliment someone. It takes being aware, knowing what good looks like, and taking a minute to say or write something positive.

During Jason's first week on the job, he accepted a dull and menial assignment. Unexpectedly, management quickly needed the results of his work. In a rush, he converted his job product into material that no one had time to review. Sensing that Jason feared for his job security, his manager said to him, "Great work, you will do just fine here."

He will never forget that experience, as the smallest of compliments meant so much to him, giving the confidence he needed to be successful at the company.

17. *Most people do not like to deal with uncertainty. When working on an assignment for which understandable direction has not been provided, do your best to clarify the situation. Being the decisive person that makes assumptions about what is expected or what should be done shows leadership that your peers and your boss appreciate.*

The Situation – embrace both: uncertainty and organized discipline

Some people, like my son, work well with and even enjoy uncertainty and ambiguity, while it literally paralyzes others who need to know the expectations for their assignment and what they are getting into. Those who enjoy uncertainty and thrive in such environments tend to be significantly more rewarded than those who do not.

On two occasions, Jason accepted newly created jobs at new companies with completely uncertain paths. In both situations, he agreed to offers without knowing his exact role. He has loved both positions and has been successful in both companies. The ambiguity helped him set the direction and the scope of his contributions.

In some ways, Carrie seems to straddle both attitudes. On the one hand, she is a successful entrepreneur who has started and built an executive recruiting business. She was effective as a management consultant by helping clients sort through ill-defined problems and opportunities. On the other hand, she has shown a desire for organized discipline in her personal life and early work.

18. *If you make a mistake, acknowledge it quickly. Do not try to cover it up. You*

risk making things worse and losing credibility. When you do not know the answer to a question (no one has all the answers), build people's confidence by admitting it rather than attempting to finesse it.

The Situation – get to trouble first, before it gets to you

In preparation for an important weekend meeting of senior management, Jason woke up one Saturday morning in a panic after realizing he had not adequately documented some material that might be discussed. Do you call and alert your boss or hope that the matter does not come up for review?

Jason called his boss, who appreciated that he had given her a "heads up." She said not to worry, as the subject was not on the agenda. From that point forward, she trusted Jason, believing she could count on him to have her back. Always try to protect your managers from unpleasant surprises.

19. *Dress for success. This advice includes good grooming. It should be obvious, but in today's world of business casual (and often far less), it needs emphasis. As a related item, observe workday etiquette; for example, punctuality, not*

> *eating breakfast at your desk, showing*
> *up a few minutes early for meetings and*
> *not distracting others (e.g., cell phone*
> *or computer). Keep your work area neat*
> *and clean. In other words, set an excel-*
> *lent example for others to follow.*

Never be the one the office talks about negatively the day after a company party or event. You don't want to be the person who was drunk, said or did something inappropriate, or did the "crazy thing" that is remembered for a long time.

The Situation – put on your best face

Despite her hope that merit was enough to determine one's success in the workplace, Carrie recognizes that amazing talent combined with inappropriate appearance does not make for success. She has always looked young for her age but never liked to wear much makeup.

While working in the trust department of a bank, her mentor (a Vice President) advised Carrie that some of her colleagues were uncomfortable putting her in front of clients (who had large trust accounts) because she looked so young. After resisting for some time, telling her mentor that her appearance should not matter if she was doing good work, Carrie recognized that some clients did not want to trust their funds to someone looking so inexperienced.

My daughter believes it is essential to dress for success. If in doubt, go for being overdressed rather than underdressed. Wear age-appropriate clothing and accessories. Factor an organization's culture into your wardrobe decisions, as Carrie did at the bank, including different and more moderate use of cosmetics. It's worth the sacrifice.

20. *Help make meetings productive by observing the process and what participants are saying. When pursuing the same objectives, reasonable people may disagree on strategies, priorities, and tactics. This requires tolerance for disagreement and an eye for how people with different positions can be brought together. Being effective in this way shortens meetings, which everyone appreciates.*

The Situation– stay on point!

In his first job, Jason loved meeting to discuss events with celebrities who anchored sports news shows. He was ready to get together all day until he learned that people, including celebrities, don't like meetings, as they can be incredibly unproductive.

As meeting leader Jason recommends: 1) define a clear reason for the meeting and tell everyone in advance 2) present an agenda and facilitate the discussion 3) let everyone know their role (note-taker, facilitator, participant) and 4) develop a plan for follow up and make sure it is executed.

Carrie believes the same guidelines should apply to phone conversations and email. Be sure to know the reason for the call and what you want from the conversation. What is the point of the email and what is your "ask"?

Chapter 5....
Be Proactive about Career Advancement

This book is about doing your job well so that you will be considered for promotion. There are other specific things you can do to take the initiative in advancing your career. Seek to be "sponsored" by executives that are clearly on the path to success. These mentors or "angels" might be in another company as well as your own. Solicit their advice and support.

Learn the skills of negotiation. Carefully plan and prepare for your next position. Here are 5 tips to help you get that next position.

> 21. *Hitch your wagon to a rising star. When you have identified someone successful and likely to advance further in their career, try to engage him or her as your*

mentor or corporate "angel." Selectively seek their advice on important issues you are facing. Let them know you are always available to help them whenever and however you can. You might be surprised how often you can help them with something. Hopefully, they will take you with them as they climb the corporate ladder.

The Situation – giddy up! Ride those coattails!

In his second job, Jason sought coaching and mentoring from a rising star. He took assignments that made life easier for his mentor and gave him credit. As the mentor rose through the organization and into new firms, he took Jason with him. My son worked for this man for almost 18 years in two companies and numerous roles. Jason was handsomely rewarded.

22. *In addition to "angels" or mentors within your company, establish relationships with executives in other companies inside your industry. You must be careful to avoid disclosing confidential information about your employer, but that need not preclude using this opportunity to learn and prepare for job openings outside of your company. Stay in touch with former employees and colleagues. Often, they*

*are a source of helpful information and
even new job possibilities.*

The Situation – build and broaden your network

This is one tip Jason wishes he had followed earlier in his career. Since I made this recommendation to Carrie and Jason, it has become much easier to execute this advice: Jason connects on LinkedIn with everyone he meets in a business context. He regularly reaches out to key contacts to touch base and compare notes on the industry and what they are doing from a career perspective.

You cannot use this approach with everyone. Use it with the "stars" who have the most upward career path and the best networks of contacts.

23. *Be prepared to take reasonable risks in your work; for example, accepting an assignment that stretches your experience and abilities. Even with failure, you can learn and improve your skills.*

The Situation – be willing to think outside the box

This is easy to say but hard to do. Early in your career, you have the least to lose by taking chances but are less likely to know the right time or situation to accept the risk. Part of knowing "when" lies in understanding your company's culture. Does it support risk, or is it risk-averse?

In his first job at a television sports network, Jason's company encouraged pushing the envelope of creativity and taking risks. While assigned to cover a relatively unimportant hockey game, Jason decided to focus on some unusual things that happened before the event (the Zamboni broke down). His reporting of the funny aspects surrounding the Zamboni, rather than the action of the game, earned praise from his boss, who explained there are thousands of games each year and it is good to do a story that is different and stands out from the crowd.

24. *Think about what you want your next job to be and carefully plan for it. Be prepared with the necessary skills and experience to hit the ground running. Hopefully, you will be the obvious candidate for the opening. As noted in #3, ideally, you should already be performing at the next level before being promoted to it.*

The Situation – learn about your next job in your current job

You can evaluate this advice from two perspectives. First, you might consider what your next role, by way of promotion, will be in your current company. The second approach requires good networking in your industry to uncover a role in a different organization. Carrie and Jason have found it easier to get more responsibility or move into a new functional area, for example, from sales to marketing, within your current company. Your employer knows you well. Moving to a new organization or industry is based on the decision-maker's view of what you have done in prior positions, rather than your potential to achieve new, more challenging objectives.

To secure a promotion in your current company it is essential to understand the requirements of the next role. Before a promotion, you will typically need to perform in that role. Before his advancement from senior consultant to manager, Jason managed a project team.

> 25. *Always keep your resume current and your eye on the next step up. Cultivate and maintain your network on a continuing basis, as these contacts may help you get the next job, whether it is inside your company or with another firm.*

The Situation – stay on top of your résumé!

As a recruiter, Carrie speaks all day with candidates, many of whom have been with their current employer for several years, assuming more responsibility during that time. If they have not done so on a regular basis, Carrie observes that they find it exceedingly difficult to recount their accomplishments and effectively update their résumé. She recommends updating every six months or so. This allows you to reflect on your accomplishments and highlight those things in your presentation. When the time comes that you need to submit a resume, you can always shorten it, if you have added too much.

26. *Develop your ability as a negotiator for your ideas, for your company, and for your job promotions and compensation. Good negotiating skills come in handy in many circumstances. There are classes and publications on negotiating. Develop a foundation of these skills and refresh them over time.*

The Situation – silence is golden

My son has used negotiating skills frequently throughout his career. He views them as essential. He considers the class on negotiating he took in business school his single most valuable training. Jason uses the knowledge learned in that class for his compensation, sales deals with customers, vendor and supplier contracts, and much more.

Carrie's customers, especially those that were new, often asked for discounts. She used "company policy" to explain her company did not discount because its rates reflect the value it provides.

Jason recalls the impact of silence as a negotiating technique. In his consulting position with a software company, Jason was responsible for setting the price of implementation services for the company's software. The sales team wanted to get the highest price possible for the software, which put pressure on the pricing of the implementation services.

Jason and the sales team were on a conference call to finalize the proposal to the customer. The sales team argued the customer could not afford the price set by Jason. After about 30 minutes of back and forth, Jason told the sales team he was firm on his price.

There was total silence for about 20 minutes. The sales team then accepted Jason's price. The customer subsequently accepted the proposal, and the silence had helped Jason to obtain higher pricing both internally and with the customer.

Chapter 6... Be Visible

Pursue recognition and visibility in your company, your industry, and other industries. Network regularly and with reciprocity. Keep your resume up to date.

> 27. *Develop relationships with potential sponsors or mentors outside of your company and industry. Professionals in consulting, finance, law, and accounting can be sources of personal advice and job opportunities. This includes executive recruiters, who will appreciate your help if you can identify qualified potential candidates for a position they seek to fill.*

The Situation – help the recruiter recruit

Both my daughter and son know the importance of having good relationships with executive recruiters. As you progress in your career, you are likely to receive calls from search firms. They value your saying upfront if you are not interested in the position they are working on and you then give them the names of other attractive candidates. Jason also maintains personal contact with recruiters to learn what they are seeing in recruiting activity, let them know what roles he might find interesting, and volunteer to assist them.

28. *Pursue recognition within your industry by attending trade shows and conferences, giving speeches and presentations at industry events, writing articles for trade publications, and participating in educational seminars. Any one of these activities may be the source of your next job offer. The contemporary method for maintaining visibility is to post thoughts and articles on LinkedIn and other social media sites.*

The Situation – be responsible for your own PR

There are many ways to achieve industry recognition. The most current is via LinkedIn. Jason and Carrie maintain connections with every one of their contacts by actively posting appropriate business content.

29. *Network regularly within and outside your industry. Build a network of friends and contacts and keep it current by an*

occasional email, phone call, or lunch meeting. These people may hear of an opportunity that would be of interest to you. Don't let the networking become one-sided. Help and recommend others whenever you can.

The Situation – maintain a personal touch

Very few young professionals recognize the importance of making time to network on a regular basis. Both Carrie and Jason believe networking is critical, and they have maintained contact with colleagues from their first and subsequent jobs. They rely on their network to connect with people they might otherwise not know. Their networks are often the source of valuable help.

Networking today is much easier using LinkedIn and other social media tools. Both Jason and Carrie stress the importance of personal contact through a phone call, a coffee, or a personal note (rather than a mass email), to stand out from the broadscale networking people do online.

Chapter 7....Be Yourself

Do not try to be someone or something you are not. Maintain the values of honesty and morality that you have learned. Have fun and enjoy your work.

> 30. *Be honest and ethical. Do the right thing. Do not compromise your principles of morality. Treat others the way you want them to treat you.*

The Situation – your reputation is your most valuable asset

Both Jason and Carrie emphasize the importance of integrity and ethics. Carrie acknowledges that some recruiters have a reputation for being transactional, unreliable, and dishonest. On contingent searches, she explains to the candidates that she has a vested interest in filling the job, but she will do her best to be objective with them. She does not suggest an opening is a good option for the candidate if this is not what she believes. As she says, this approach may cost her money; but she sleeps better at night. Many candidates have told her that working with her is a different and better experience than other recruiters and much appreciated.

Jason says, "all you have is your reputation," and it is much easier to destroy a reputation than to build it.

Jason and Carrie know examples of colleagues who bent the rules for their personal benefit. In their early days of business travel, both had associates who suggested they ask for several blank taxi receipts that they could fill in and submit later. With Uber and similar options, this scam may be less frequent, but plenty of substitutes exist. The practice is unethical, amounting to fraud and theft.

31. *Don't try to fit a stereotype or be someone or something that does not come naturally. People sense this acting. Ultimately, you will become uncomfortable with yourself and risk losing your credibility and self-confidence.*

The Situation – be the person who knows you best: YOU

Often younger people starting out find it challenging to know and have confidence in who they are and how to be themselves. My son says if you enjoy doing a certain task or activity, do more of it. Your passion and excitement will come through in the work you do, and others will recognize it.

Do not try to be someone you are not. Jason learned he was not good at telling jokes at the beginning of a presentation, as many public speakers do. Instead, he started using quotes that sometimes were humorous (without a joke) and allowed him to stay on message. Beginning a presentation with a good start gave him confidence.

32. *Maintain your sense of humor. Don't get too serious.*

The Situation

Jason believes the key to keeping a sense of humor is to enjoy your job. In his first position, he usually worked 60 or more hours during a six-day week. I suspect he has put in that much time in all of his assignments. He said that humor must be appropriate for the context and the audience. As he progressed in his career and became a team leader, he has used humor to ensure the culture is not too serious.

41

Chapter 8....Be Real

Stay healthy, both mentally and physically. No smoking or drugs. Alcohol in moderation. Respect the norms regarding gender and sex in both your actions and your conversations. Above all, maintain a proper focus on your family and keep a balance between family and work.

33. *Always maintain a positive attitude. People do not want to know about your personal problems or see such issues influencing your attitude or the quality of your work.*

The Situation – stay PSE – Positive, Sharp, Enthusiastic

While this advice might seem obvious, people too often fail to follow it. Most people, particularly those in management, want to work with associates who have a positive and enthusiastic attitude. No one enjoys being around anyone in a bad mood, who doesn't like their work or frequently talks about personal issues. At his first company, Jason knew a bright and talented colleague who did not progress beyond his probation period because he was always in a grim frame of mind and rarely had anything positive to say. Teammates did not want to work with him.

34. *Stay healthy. Eat right and exercise. Both help the brain and the body. Avoid smoking and keep the alcohol consumption moderate, especially in business-related settings. No drugs. Though you should expect to work long hours in your first job, you still need to balance work with your social life and community involvement.*

The Situation – stay healthy, stay fit, stay smart

My son confessed that during his first job he did a poor job of taking care of himself. "Eating right" meant one trip to McDonald's and no less than 2 liters of Coca-Cola each day. He limited exercise to occasional basketball games, in which he was able to develop relationships with members of senior management.

Jason's first job involved odd hours, with his colleagues often working until two or three in the morning and then going to someone's home to drink until sunrise.

Although not a specific part of my advice, Jason knew that you should never drink on the job or arrive at work drunk. One day one of his colleagues showed up drunk, smelling of alcohol. Jason helped him to avoid detection by performing his friend's job and his own. The colleague did not survive his six-month trial period.

35. *As you advance professionally and start a family, the workday is unlikely to get shorter. Pay attention to your family. Keep your work and personal lives in balance. You need the enjoyment that comes from good family life and the support the family gives you, especially when things get rough on the job. The hours not spent with spouse and children can never be recovered.*

The Situation – all work and no play makes you a bore

Most people starting in entry-level positions do not have a family to support and spend time with. Jason interpreted this advice as achieving balance in his life, which is difficult when you devote so many hours to the job. Even early in his career, he found it useful to take time from work to clear his mind.

As he got older, Jason made a conscious effort to spend time with family and friends. When he stops on

Friday evening, he tries to avoid anything job-related until Sunday morning. This gives him 36 hours with family, friends, and himself. He believes colleagues, clients, and contacts understand and respect his approach. He is confident you can pull away from work if you set your mind to do it.

36. *Be aware of and sensitive to current values and organizational policies regarding conversations and behavior related to gender and sex. A touch here, a pat there, a term of endearment, humor in poor taste, or more may be considered inappropriate. Stick to the business.*

The Situation – stick to your moral values

The MeToo movement has brought this advice to the forefront. Carrie and Jason began their careers in a different environment. During my son's first job, he attended a party of about 15 people at a company executive's home. At one point, the executive took a young female employee on a one-to-one tour of his residence. Jason and a colleague happened to walk by and see the executive getting a little too close to the woman. She looked uncomfortable. Jason and his friend joined them for a few minutes and then invited the woman to reconnect with the group. This may have prevented an inappropriate situation … or much worse.

Conclusion....Be Alert

Be alert to opportunities and pitfalls that frequently arise during your career. You know what you say and do affects how people react to you and what they think of you. This book has hopefully stimulated you to be aware of the many ways such interactions can be important to personal success in your work environment.

You may not recall these tips on a day-to-day basis or when you act. However, if they help to form good instincts, you will succeed.

As you progress through your career, you will have new perspectives on this book's contents and its relevance to your work. You should do a quick review of the book annually, and whenever you accept new responsibilities, to refresh your instincts.

Good luck.

Final Words of Wisdom from My Children

From Jason Kurtz:

My father gave me this set of guidelines when I was 22 and about to start my first job at ESPN. As you can imagine, it was a time of mixed emotions for me. On the one hand, I was excited to become more independent and to achieve a dream of working in sports television. On the other hand, I had a lot of insecurity about being good enough to meet the ESPN standard. And, Bristol, Connecticut was a depressing place in 1990. I grew up in Miami, Florida and went to college in Austin, Texas. Bristol could not have been more different than those two amazing cities. I remember looking for apartments and my father and I sitting in a mall wondering if we should just drive home to Miami and forget the ESPN opportunity. Fortunately, I decided to stick it out. I don't remember the exact moment Dad gave me his letter (everything from Dad comes in the

form of a letter from him to my sister or me). I do remember reading it – I am pretty sure internally I did
a bit of an "eye roll," but externally, I remember an
emotional moment with Dad filled with a big hug and
some tears. I also remember reading the letter a few
times the evening before my first day at work.

As I have mentioned to my father, his letter was not
something I referred to on a regular basis. However,
I feel like the advice stays in the back of my mind –
almost in my subconscious. I do not think there were
many days where I would stop and say to myself, "I
wonder what Dad's advice would say about this situation." I do believe the suggestions became a part of
my intuitive value system for considering what to do
and how to handle various circumstances. They became a part of whatever I did. As I look back at the
letter now, it is amazing to me to see how much of it I
put into practice. I can provide examples of how I applied each and every one of Dad's recommendations.

Over time, I shared the list with a few friends and
colleagues. Each said the advice is fantastic and how
lucky I am to have a father who could provide such
excellent guidance. They're absolutely right – thanks,
Dad, for everything you've provided me, for always
being there for me, and of course, for these suggestions. You're the best – I love you!

From Carrie Kurtz Turner:

I'm not sure when my Dad first gave me his list of guidelines for my first job, but I know it has stuck with me throughout my career and personal life. Growing up, my parents taught (and showed by example) the importance of self-discipline, integrity, and humility. So, when I read through my Dad's advice, it's no surprise that these values are woven throughout his words. I know that every step of the way in my career, I have been guided by the principles that are outlined in this book. In fact, I would say my personal life is also guided by my Dad's advice about making the most of your job. Be a team player, be a listener, be a star, be a leader, be proactive, be visible, be yourself, and be real. These are all guiding principles that I call upon daily, whether I'm at work or parenting a child, or talking to my husband about his day. I don't need my Dad's piece of paper to remind me of how to live my best life, but it's nice to have it handy for a reminder now and again!

Recently as I was working to develop new marketing materials for my recruiting business, I turned again to what my Dad taught me. I was able to sum up my Dad's advice as "traditional values applied to today's modern world." My Dad has set the bar high for a life well led both personally and professionally. I am fortunate to have had a lifetime of his guidance, and now you, the reader, can benefit from his experience as well.

Appendix

A brief timeline of the education and career history of Ron, Jason, and Carrie.

Ron Kurtz

The University of Texas at Austin BBA and BJ 1964

Ford Motor Co., Marketing Research Analyst 1964-1965

Harvard Graduate School of Business, MBA 1967, and Research Assistant 1967-1968

Northeast Airlines, Director of Marketing Research and Planning 1968-1970

Pan American Airways, Staff Vice President 1970-1973

The French Line, Chief Marketing Officer 1973 to 1974

Quality Inns (Now Choice Hotels), Vice President of Marketing 1975-1976

American Express Travel Division, Vice President of Travel Products 1976-1979

Norwegian Caribbean Lines (now Norwegian Cruise Line), Senior Vice President Marketing and Sales 1980 to 1982

Sea Goddess Cruises, President 1982-1986

Windstar Cruises, Senior Vice President 1987-1989

Management Resource Group, Owner 1989-2002

American Affluence Research Center, Owner 2002 to present

Jason Kurtz

The University of Texas at Austin BBA and BJ 1990

The University of Virginia, Darden Graduate School of Business MBA 1995

ESPN 1990-93; Associate Producer

Arthur Andersen Business Consulting 1995-2002; Director

Ariba, Inc 2002 – 2013 Vice President and General Manager

Accel-KKR 2013 – Present – Managing Director

Carrie Kurtz Turner

Cornell BA 1994

Chicago Booth MBA 2001

First Chicago Bank (now Chase) 1994-1999, Project Manager

BearingPoint 2002-2006, Consulting Manager and Recruiting Manager

Socium Group LLC Co-Founder/Managing Partner, 2008- Present

Notes from Colleagues Who Worked with the Author

From Helge Naarstad (My Supervisor in 3 Different Environments)

I had the privilege to work with Ron over a period of almost 10 years. First in the capacity of his position as Senior VP marketing/sales for Norwegian Caribbean Lines, where I served as President and then as President of SeaGoddess Cruises, where I was the Chairman of the Board.

Ron is very knowledgeable, has great insight in the cruise industry and is a master of market techniques .

On a personal basis he is great with words, communicates very distinctly and explains situations in precise and comprehensive language. He is loyal, makes good analysis, is friendly, convincing, keeps his position in discussions, but may still carry out decisions he is not totally in favor of.

Ron is very professional and he keeps thinking and analyzing ideas and problems, till he finds a solution that will satisfy his professional training, but also keeping in mind that solutions sometimes require elements of compromise and practicality. To do that, without compromising on his character, requires never letting the goal out of sight, and sometimes the longest road is the only feasible. To me this describes an analytical mind, but also a doer. A person who can carry out a complicated plan, but with dignity and resolution.

I like to think that we through the years developed not only mutual respect, but also friendship.

Ron has a good sense of humor, which I found entertaining, even in the most trying of circumstances.

He is a good friend and I miss seeing him.

From Susan Kelley (Who worked with me in 3 Different Environments)

*You have always exuded the very highest standards.

The counter side is that your level of trust was in the questionable category – double, triple checking everything. (the red pen syndrome).

*You always showed respect for people and listened to people even to the less talented folk.

*You were always approachable probably due to your somewhat laid-back disposition.

*I recall you worked incredible hours.

From Terry Thornton (Who I Hired in 3 Different Companies)

Ron and I initially worked together at Norwegian Caribbean Lines (now Norwegian Cruise Line) where I was a junior member of the finance and marketing teams. We later worked more closely together during the startup of Sea Goddess Cruises Limited.

During my NCL days, I remember thinking how innovative some of Ron's initiatives were, including the marketing approach with network television, unique pricing and promotions, early efforts to more clearly differentiate the NCL brand and many other initiatives. Reflecting on this, I was able to broaden my thinking about the NCL business model and began to understand how important these initiatives were in driving improvements for the brand.

At Sea Goddess, it was an exciting time to actually launch an innovative new small ship luxury brand. The nature of a start-up is the unique ability to work on many aspects of the business even though my focus was the financial area. This allowed me to understand much more about the overall business from the ship design, marine operations, onboard product, sales and marketing and shoreside operations. Working closely with Ron, it instilled a much deeper sense and appreciation for an extremely strong work ethic. Ron also allowed me to be involved in so many aspects of the business that created an unprecedented level of learning in a very short period of time. Because of this, I have seen the power of working hard and pushing through challenges to achieve my goals. I have also learned the power of involving members of my teams in a variety of learning experiences to help them grow and become more significant contributors to the company success.

From Emilio Freeman (Who Worked with and for Me in Two Different Environments).

I have known Ron Kurtz for over 40 years and consider him a true friend and mentor. These feelings have been solidified and reinforced over the years. Like many other leaders I have worked with before, Ron has provided direction, insight, counsel, and professional opinions, but always with a unique style of humility and honesty – i.e., a trait few others manifest. Ron was (is) always sensitive and cognizant to how the message is received.

Over the years I admired Ron's approach to leadership a lot and tried to mirror that approach in my own career and with my own children. I learned that like the old adage, "you can lead a horse to water but you can't make it drink," you must speak and listen in a way that the other person can relate to and be sensitive to not offend. This is exactly how my dealings with Ron were.

There are many examples I could cite about Ron's strong yet humble character but one that always, always touched me greatly was September 11th, 2001. We all remember that day. For me, I was driving to work that Tuesday morning, to go to work listening to Howard Stern on the radio. As I was getting ready to get out of the car, the news of the first attack was broadcast. I sat there in my car for about 30 minutes listening in horror and realized I needed to go to work. When I walked in the office no one knew about what was happening. It was a regular day at ResidenSea – the company where Ron and I both worked.

I immediately walked into the conference room and turned the TV on and continued to watch with horror. Other staff members joined in and we were all in shock. By 10am I knew I needed to start the workday and went to see Ron in his office. He was busy preparing a report and asked me why I was late. My words were something like "Ron, do you know what happened in New York? It seems that at terrorist attack has taken place and many people are hurt." I think Ron only half heard what I said and was preoccupied with work. I walked away in shock as to his disregard to the situation.

(Please note this Ron was not the Ron I normally interacted with, but given the situation at that time with our company, there were many intense projects going on at that time and Ron, through his normal focused intensity, did not easily let the outside world interfere with the matters on that specific day).

The next day, first thing in the morning Ron came to my office, closed the door, sat down, and said to me "Emilio, I am very sorry about my insensitivity yesterday. I had no idea about what happened until I watched TV last night. It was horrible and I hope you accept my apology for not recognizing the magnitude of your concern and hurt." I was surprised but comforted to know that Ron could see through me and be humble about his oversight. Someone else might have chosen to ignore their own error and move on.

As stated earlier, few leaders can be both strong and humble at the same time, but I can say Ron is one of those few. He was able to put aside his corporate rank hierarchical and spoke as a friend and recognized his insensitivity. I always respected that, always admired knowing that Ron's even-keeled approach to work and awareness of feelings were traits I wanted to emulate. Never boisterous, never overbearing, always honest, always humble. – a true gentle giant.

About the Author

 After starting his career in the airline industry, Ron became President of two cruise lines and Chief Marketing and Sales officer of two others. He was a corporate executive for 20 years and a management consultant for 14 years.

Ron earned his MBA from Harvard and BBA and BJ degrees at the University of Texas.

https://www.linkedin.com/in/ronald-kurtz-63b8162/

9 781977 245823